Visions of Wimbledon

Visions of Wimbledon

A CELEBRATION OF

THE WORLD'S FINEST WIMBLEDON PHOTOGRAPHY

BY THE ALLSPORT PHOTOGRAPHIC AGENCY

ANDRE
DEUTSCH

≈ The Photograph Shows ≈
1974

Bjorn Borg (Sweden),
the teeny-boppers' idol, enters
the court for his match against
Ross Case (Australia), watched
by his admiring young fans.

≈

First published in 2000 by
André Deutsch Ltd
76 Dean Street
London W1V 5HA

www.vci.co.uk

A CIP catalogue record for this book
is available from the British Library

ISBN 0 233 99868 3

Text by: Andrew Longmore

Design by: Robert Kelland

Picture Editors: Clive Brunskill and Gary M Prior
Picture Editor/ Research: Elaine Lobo

Special thanks to Phillip Burnham-Richards at Hulton Getty, Ian Edwards at
The AELTC and all at the Wimbledon Lawn Tennis Museum.

This book has been made possible with the generous support and assistance
of Canon Europa n.v.

Printed in Italy by Officine Grafiche DeAgostini

Net detail (half-title page)
PHOTOGRAPH BY GARY M PRIOR

Pete Sampras, 1999 (frontispiece)
PHOTOGRAPH BY GARY M PRIOR

Wimbledon motif, 1998 (title page)
PHOTOGRAPH BY MIKE HEWITT

Bjorn Borg, 1974 (left)
PHOTOGRAPH ALLSPORT HISTORICAL COLLECTION © HULTON GETTY

Aerial view of Wimbledon, June 1999 (above)
HRH The Duke and Duchess of Kent with Cedric Piolene, July 1997 (opposite)

PHOTOGRAPHS BY GARY M PRIOR

FOREWORD

by HRH The Duke of Kent
President, All England Club

In 1929 Prince George became President of the All England Club and began my family's connection with Wimbledon. This association was continued by my mother, the Duchess of Kent, who attended The Championships for twenty-three successive years. I presented the men's singles trophy for the first time to Rod Laver in 1969 and since then I have had the honour and privilege of watching and congratulating successive Champions, men and women, each one with a different character and different qualities. One of the beauties of the game and one of the qualities that makes it so photogenic is that it reveals personality as well as prowess.

I have often wondered how the Champions of the past would have compared with modern professionals. The development of racket technology and the standard of fitness have made the game faster and more athletic. And media interest has also grown enormously. No twitch, shot or expression goes unrecorded now and the standard of photography, in particular, has developed in parallel with the game, as the pictures in this book so graphically illustrate. I marvel at the ability of a photographer to capture the emotion of the moment.

Yet Wimbledon itself, with its traditions, its architecture, its contrasting colours, distinctive atmosphere and of course its varied weather conditions must provide the ideal canvas for the photographer. The tournament is the highlight of my sporting summer. Now I can open this book and experience the essence of Wimbledon all year round. I am delighted to be associated with *Visions of Wimbledon* and wish the photographers at Allsport and the publication every success.

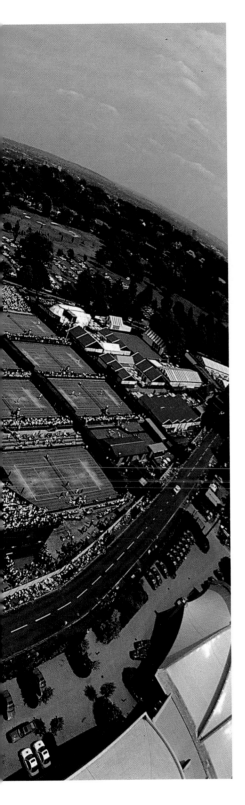

Church Road, undated (above)
PHOTOGRAPH WIMBLEDON LAWN TENNIS MUSEUM

Aerial view of the All England Lawn Tennis Championships, 1993 (left)
PHOTOGRAPH BY SIMON BRUTY

INTRODUCTION

by Andrew Longmore for Allsport Photographic

Tennis, in any setting, lends itself to the camera. The power of Sampras and the athleticism of Navratilova are matched by the guile of Graf and the mischief of Nastase. The camera captures and distils a game of subtlety, rhythm and character down to a single moment. Yet only at Wimbledon does the setting match the drama. The backdrop is instantly recognizable, from the intimacy of Centre Court to the strawberries and cream, and the creeper that decorates the walls of the clubhouse. Wimbledon is a star in its own right, and burns brighter than any of those whose skills adorn the courts for two weeks each summer. Those who tread the sacred turf are well aware that they are merely actors on the grandest stage of all. The magic of Wimbledon will be there long after they have retired to tell grandchildren of their triumphs.

In the following pages you will find most of the great Champions and many of the great moments in Wimbledon's history. However, this is not a history book, nor a photographic record of a unique institution. It is a book to prompt reflection and nostalgia, a book that showcases both the players that act out the drama and the photographers who capture the moment so instinctively. The photographers thrive on the emotion of their subject. They want to see Becker's exuberance, the tearful Novotna and the tempestuous McEnroe. The moment must be captured; and it is not just the players that feel the pressure of Wimbledon Fortnight. The photographers must also endure the weight of expectation in order to provide the best.

Collected here are the visions of Wimbledon. They are images that encapsulate every aspect of the premier event on the tennis calendar. From the tension of Centre Court battles to the upsets of the outside courts, Allsport's photographers have captured it all. Accompanying these images are testimonies from some of the great Champions of Wimbledon, past and present. Players such as Stefan Edberg, Martina Navratilova and Rod Laver recount their Wimbledon experiences, both good and bad. For these players Centre Court became their second home, a place in which they were able to relax despite the pressure. However, memories are not restricted to the showpiece courts. There are tales of the outside courts that host much of the drama and alongside are the stories of those behind the success of the tournament, the fans and the staff. For them, like the players themselves, Wimbledon truly is the highlight of any year.

Throughout the years the structure of Wimbledon has changed. Developments such as the new Number 1 Court have been built in order to keep up with the ever-increasing demands from fans, players and media alike. Despite these changes however, one thing remains, the spirit of Wimbledon. It is a spirit that has grown through years of triumph and despair, of tears and tantrums. The Champions move on, Wimbledon remains. This book is a celebration of that spirit.

Mary Pierce, 1995 (left)
PHOTOGRAPH BY CLIVE BRUNSKILL

Waiting for Play

Building work on Centre Court, 1978 (left)
PHOTOGRAPH ALLSPORT HISTORICAL COLLECTION
© HULTON GETTY

*Removing the turf from the old
No 1 Court, 1996* (centre left)
PHOTOGRAPH BY GRAHAM CHADWICK

The new No 1 Court, 1996
(bottom left and right)
PHOTOGRAPH BY GARY M PRIOR

*Bunny Austin, Dan Maskell and
Helen Wills Moody, undated*
('Waiting for play', pages 12-13)
PHOTOGRAPH ALLSPORT HISTORICAL COLLECTION
© HULTON GETTY

Waiting for Play

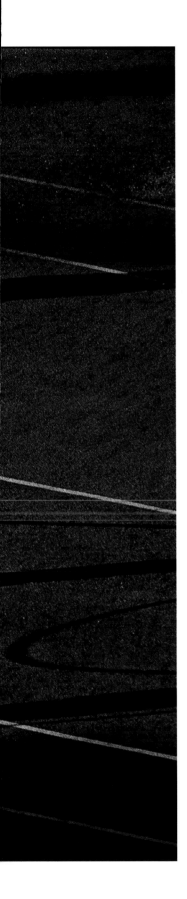

≈ The Photograph Shows ≈
1961

Another Wimbledon.
For the first time in thirty-five years, the famous Centre Court (above)
at Wimbledon is being re-turfed instead of re-sown, in the belief that this will strengthen
the court's resistance to wear. Sods cut from the court surrounds – which will be re-sown –
are being transplanted. Mr R Twyman, assistant groundsman at Wimbledon, carefully
places a sod into position and with tender fingers makes sure it is level.

≈

Turf laying, 1961 (above)
PHOTOGRAPH ALLSPORT HISTORICAL COLLECTION © HULTON GETTY

Watering the courts, 1995 (left)
PHOTOGRAPH BY MICHAEL COOPER

Rolling the court, 1963 (top)

Putting up the net, undated (above)

Visions of Wimbledon

MY WIMBLEDON

by Eddie Seaward
Head Groundsman, All England Club

When the spring comes, it's like flicking a switch. The Club comes alive, we're into The Championships and there's an air of real bustle about the place again. It makes my pulse quicken. At Christmas, you think: 'Oh yes, twenty-five weeks to The Championships. Plenty of time.' Then, it's sixteen weeks. Fine. All of a sudden, it's six days. Time just slips away. We feel that every year.

As I get nearer the tournament, I get almost paranoid about the grass. I see a mark on a court, it's nothing really, but I go home on Friday and, in my head, by Monday morning a little scuff mark has grown to the size of a crater. But that's the right way for it to be. We are always looking for perfection, always striving. The colour of the grass, the wear, the consistency – there's always something that can be improved for the following year. I walk on the Centre Court every day and just by walking on certain patches I can tell if there are any problems. If one bit is wet, I know how wet the rest of the court will be. It's not something you can learn from a textbook, it just comes from experience. But I try not just to concentrate on Centre Court, I want every court to be just right.

As The Championships get near, my life is dominated by the weather forecast. It becomes fanatical, almost destructive because we can't do anything about it. You just have to take what comes. The ideal pattern for us is to get quite a lot of rain about a month before the start of The Championships, to get the moisture down into the grass and then have a week's sunshine before the tournament starts. Our job is made much easier if it's dry during the fortnight and even if rain sets in for

the day, at least we know what's going on. The nightmare is one of those overcast, showery days when the covers are always coming on and off and you get neck ache looking at the sky trying to anticipate what's coming next. We can cover the Centre Court in twenty-eight seconds, but the trick is to get the covers on just before the rain sets in. A day like that is tiring for us and utterly frustrating for the spectators, who haven't paid to watch us.

Mostly, during the Fortnight, I will be keeping an eye on Centre Court. Sometimes I will nip up to the referee's office to see what's happening elsewhere on the closed circuit television. But I've got good, experienced staff and they know what to do, so I don't feel as if I have to be everywhere at once. The best moment of the Fortnight for me is when the final point has been played in the last match and everything has run smoothly. But it's only a matter of days before we're talking about what can be done to make it better next year.

I used to queue up to get into The Championships and never believed for a moment that I would work here. The beauty of the place can still take your breath away; in the autumn the creeper turns red and the clubhouse looks magnificent. The public doesn't see Wimbledon so much then – they see it when the place is green. It's a magical place, there's no doubt about it. The whole atmosphere, the whole feeling of it, even on cold, wet winter days. I can get blasé about Centre Court, but when you take visitors onto the court and see the wonder in their eyes, it reminds you how much it means to them and how privileged I am to be working here. To me it's not a job, it's a way of life.

*Scene of crime officers remove samples of painted turf
from the Centre Court, January 1976* (above)

PHOTOGRAPH ALLSPORT HISTORICAL COLLECTION © HULTON GETTY

Groundsman mows the Centre Court, 1994 (right)

PHOTOGRAPH BY GARY M PRIOR

'Wimbledon is foremost a national phenomenon. In fact, I think it can be argued that Wimbledon captures the imagination of a complete country more than any other athletic event in the world.'

ARTHUR ASHE
(PORTRAIT IN MOTION, 1975)

Fans queuing overnight for Saturday tickets, 1993 (left, top and bottom)
PHOTOGRAPHS BY MICHAEL COOPER

Camping out in the rain, 1979 (left centre)
The Mobile Buffet, 1937 (right)
PHOTOGRAPHS ALLSPORT HISTORICAL COLLECTION
© HULTON GETTY

≈ The Photograph Shows ≈
1937

Early morning scenes at Wimbledon.
An innovation amongst the usual early morning queues at Wimbledon for the
opening of the Championships today was the latest mobile buffet
shown in demand this morning.

≈

Waiting for Play

≈ The Photograph Shows ≈
1950

A busker entertains queues waiting to see Australian Frank Sedgman's Mens' Singles Final match
against Budge Patty of the USA at Wimbledon.

≈

Visions of Wimbledon

MY WIMBLEDON

by Richard Hess
Californian spectator

On the Sunday before The Championships, I set up my tent on the pavement. There tends to be the same faces around you, people you've met from the previous years. I have an inflatable mattress and a sleeping bag and once the tent is up, I keep myself pretty warm and dry. It's hard to get more than five hours' sleep because you never get the tent set up until 11pm and the traffic starts in the early hours. I first came in 1978 and I've been coming pretty much each year for twenty years now, each day, every day. I know the names of many of the stewards now, so they give me a little special treatment.

Queuing is part of the Wimbledon experience, part of my own family life too. My wife usually travels with me, all my children have come with me at different times and for The Millennium Championships my eldest daughter will be bringing her children for a week. So it will be a sort of family reunion. I'm retired, so I take my holidays every summer and come to Wimbledon.

I love tennis anyway. I still play four times a week back in the States, at the age of fifty-five, but I love Wimbledon in particular. I like the English sense of tradition and I like the more intellectual sense of humour. There is an intimacy and a history at Wimbledon that is different from the other tournaments and, strangely enough, an openness too. If you are willing to queue you can get front row seats on Centre Court every day, which is not possible at the French or the Australian Opens. It's just a shame they did away with the standing room areas on Centre and Number 1 Courts because we had lots of fun there.

I've seen so many great players on Centre Court, it's hard to pick out one or two. I like the players with character: Nastase, Connors, McEnroe and Agassi. In my ideal world, Connors would meet Agassi in the Wimbledon Final. That would be explosive one way or another. I also like contrasting styles: Sampras v Connors would be a great match.

But being a follower of US college tennis – I once played Dennis Ralston, the former Wimbledon finalist at college – I like to watch the college kids and see how they do. Every morning, I get the order of play and underline matches I must see and matches I would like to see. There is a subtle difference.

I look forward to coming back each year, for the tennis and to meet new people. I'm in the south queue. I'll be the only one wearing a shirt and tie. So you can't miss me.

Wimbledon crowds, 1950 (opposite)

Waiting for Play

❝Wimbledon, it means more
than just winning, you know,
for me. After a number
of years, it was always
important to be back and
be part of the tournament
and to do well. Since only
one person can win it,
you know, you still have
to enjoy it.
I had a great time.❞

BORIS BECKER
REFLECTING ON HIS WIMBLEDON CAREER.

*The Wimbledon tennis special,
undated* (right top)
Tea on the lawns, 1905
(right centre)
PHOTOGRAPHS
WIMBLEDON LAWN TENNIS MUSEUM

Spectators, 1914 (right bottom)
PHOTOGRAPH ALLSPORT HISTORICAL
COLLECTION © HULTON GETTY

Spectators, 1934 (opposite)
PHOTOGRAPH
WIMBLEDON LAWN TENNIS MUSEUM

‘Of all the evocative names in sports... I do not believe that any has more significance

or rings the bells of memory more loudly and clearly than Wimbledon.’

HERBERT WARREN WIND

Waiting for Play

MISS M. PIERCE	6-3 6-2		
Miss P. SCHNYDER	Miss C. TAYLOR	Miss M. PIERCE	
Miss J. WARD	6-3 6-2	6-4 6-2	Miss M. PIERCE
Miss C. TAYLOR	Miss R. HIRAKI	v	6-4 6-1
Miss R. HIRAKI	7-5 6-4	Miss N. MEDVEDEVA	
Miss C. SINGER	Miss N. MEDVEDEVA	6-3 6-2	v
Miss C. MORARIU	5-7 7-5 6-4		
Miss N. MEDVEDEVA	Miss E. LIKHOVTSEVA	Miss E. LIKHOVTSEVA	
Miss E. LIKHOVTSEVA	7-6 6-3	6-4 6-3	Miss E. LIKHOVTSEVA
Miss E.S.H. CALLENS	Miss K. ADAMS		6-3 4-6 6-0
Miss A. GAVALDON	7-6 6-1	Mrs L. NEILAND	
Miss K.M. ADAMS	Mrs L. NEILAND	6-3 6-2	
Mrs L. NEILAND	6-3 6-3		
Miss K.S. RINALDI STUNKEL	Miss L.A. DAVENPORT		
Miss M. SCHNELL	6-4 6-1	Miss J. WIESNER	
Miss L.A. DAVENPORT	Miss J. WIESNER	6-2 6-3	Miss J. WIESNER
Miss K. HABSUDOVA	6-0 7-5	v	6-2 7-5
Mrs J.K. WIESNER	Miss M. PAZ		
Mrs M. WERDEL WITMEYER	6-4 6-4	Miss G. FERNANDEZ	v
Miss M. PAZ	Miss G. PIZZICHINI	6-2 6-1	
Miss K. NOWAK	6-0 6-2		
Miss G. PIZZICHINI	Miss G.FERNANDEZ		
Miss.T. JECMENICA	2-6 6-3 6-4	Miss A. FRAZIER	
Miss G. FERNANDEZ	Miss S-H. PARK	6-4 6-1	Miss A. FRAZIER
Miss R. ZRUBAKOVA	6-2 6-2	v	6-0 6-3
Miss S-H. PARK	Miss A. FRAZIER		
Miss A. FRAZIER	6-3 6-1	Miss I. GORROCHATEGUI	
Miss D. RANDRIANTEFY	Miss I. GORROCHATEGUI	6-3 2-6 6-4	
Miss I. GORROCHATEGUI	6-4 7-5		
Miss A. SMASHNOVA	Miss I. SPIRLEA		
Miss S. SMITH	3-6 6-1 6-2	Mrs B. SCHULTZ-McCARTHY	
Miss I. SPIRLEA	Miss B. SCHULTZ-McCARTHY	6-3 6-0	Miss S. APPLEMANS
Mrs B. SCHULTZ-McCARTHY	6-0 6-3	v	7-5 2-6 12-10
Miss J. KRUGER	Miss J. WATANABE		
Miss R. BOBKOVA	6-3 6-3	Miss S. APPLEMANS	v
Miss J. WATANABE	Miss A. OLSZA	6-3 6-1	
Miss A. OLSZA	6-3 6-4		
Miss M. GRZYBOWSKA	Miss S. APPELMANS		
Miss N. MIYAGI	6-3 6-4	Miss N. SAWAMATSU	
Miss S. APPELMANS	Miss F. PERFETTI	6-4 6-0	
Miss F. PERFETTI	4-6 6-2 11-9		
Mrs M. SANCHEZ LORENZO	Miss N. SAWAMATSU		Miss A. SANCHEZ VICARIO
Miss N. SAWAMATSU	7-6 6-2	Miss A. SANCHEZ VICARIO	6-4 6-1
Miss N.K. KIJIMUTA	Miss M. OREMANS	7-5 6-3	
Miss M. OREMANS	7-6 6-3		
Miss R. GRANDE	Miss A. SANCHEZ VICARIO		
Miss A. SERRA-ZANETTI	6-3 6-4		
Miss A. SANCHEZ VICARIO	Miss A. HUBER	Miss A. HUBER	
Miss A. HUBER	6-1 6-1	6-2 6-1	
Miss G. LEON GARCIA	Miss P.H. SHRIVER		Miss A. SUGIYAMA
Miss P.H. SHRIVER	6-4 6-4		7-6 6-1
Miss A. ELLWOOD	Miss H. SUKOVA		
Miss K. GODRIDGE	6-3 6-3	Miss A. SUGIYAMA	v
Miss H. SUKOVA	Miss A. SUGIYAMA	6-4 6-1	
Miss A. KREMER	7-5 6-4		
Miss A. SUGIYAMA	Miss B. SCHETT		
Miss P. BEGEROW	4-6 6-2 6-3		
Miss B. SCHETT	Miss F. LABAT	Miss F. LABAT	
Miss F. LABAT	6-1 2-6 7-5	6-2 2-6 6-2	Miss M.J. FERNANDEZ
Mrs T.S. WHITLINGER JONES	Miss S. TESTUD		6-2 6-0
Miss S. CACIC	6-1 6-3	Miss M.J. FERNANDEZ	
Miss S. TESTUD	Miss M.J. FERNANDEZ	6-2 6-0	
Miss J. KANDARR			

≈ The Photograph Shows ≈
1932

Ellsworth Vines, the young American champion, who is to make his first appearance at Wimbledon next week, will compete in the London Lawn Tennis Championships at Queen's Club this week. Vines (taller) walks off the court with Mr Maskell, the professional champion (right).

≈

The draw, 1996 (above)

PHOTOGRAPH BY STU FORSTER

Ellsworth Vines at Wimbledon, 1932 (right)

The draw, 1934 (opposite)

PHOTOGRAPHS ALLSPORT HISTORICAL COLLECTION
© HULTON GETTY

Waiting for Play

It's enclosed, yet it's outdoors. You have the feeling of being in a shrine. No other place in the world can duplicate this feeling. Wimbledon is special.

CHRIS EVERT
THREE TIMES WIMBLEDON CHAMPION,
ON THE CENTRE COURT. (CHRISSIE, 1982)

(Opposite,
clockwise from top left)
*G Von Cramm and
J Drobny, 1951*
*Mrs Kitty Godfree (right) and
Signorita D'Alvarez, 1926*
*Mrs F J Bartlett (Australia) and
Miss C Proctor (South Africa)
going out for the match
against Miss Nancy Chaffee
and Miss B Baker (USA) on
Centre Court, 1951*
PHOTOGRAPHS ALLSPORT HISTORICAL
COLLECTION © HULTON GETTY

Chris Evert, 1980 (right)
PHOTOGRAPH BY TONY DUFFY

Play!

(Clockwise from top left) *Pete Sampras, 1992*

PHOTOGRAPH BY CHRIS COLE

Ball-boy, 1987

PHOTOGRAPH BY CHRIS COLE

Shadow serve, 1997

PHOTOGRAPH BY STU FORSTER

Ball-boy, 1995

PHOTOGRAPH BY CLIVE BRUNSKILL

Wayne Ferreira, 1995 (left)

PHOTOGRAPH BY CLIVE MASON

Courts 3, 4 and 5, 1995
('Play', pages 32-3)

PHOTOGRAPH BY MICHAEL COOPER

Play!

Fred Perry, 1935 (opposite)

John McEnroe, 1984 (above left)

Frank Shields, 1931 (above right)

Pete Sampras, 1998 (opposite)
Karsten Braasch, 1995 (above)
PHOTOGRAPHS BY GARY M PRIOR

N Pietrangeli and ball-boy, 1958 (right)

PHOTOGRAPH ALLSPORT HISTORICAL COLLECTION © HULTON GETTY

Boris Becker and ball-boy, 1991 (below)

PHOTOGRAPH BY BOB MARTIN

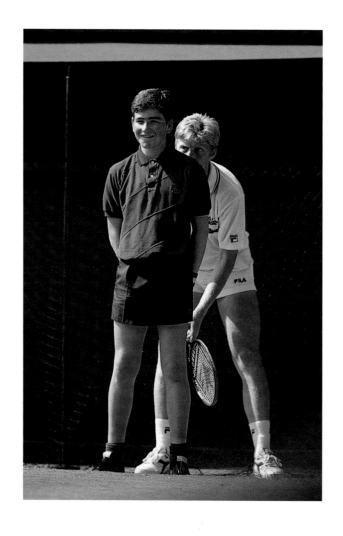

MY WIMBLEDON

by Tim Henman
British Number One

I first visited Wimbledon in 1980. I went with my mother to watch Borg and McEnroe in that epic five-set final, which Borg won. It was a defining moment. I decided there and then that this was the game for me and this was where I wanted to play. There was already an historical relationship between the Henman family and Wimbledon; my great-grandmother, Ellen Stawell-Brown, was the first lady to serve overarm at The Championships and my grandfather, Henry Billington, played in the forties and fifties, but these were still heady ambitions for a five-year-old.

The strange thing was that when I first came to play on Centre Court, against Yevgeny Kafelnikov, in the first round of The 1996 Championships, I felt as if I had been preparing for the moment all my life. I'd sat up in the stands before the match for fifteen minutes just soaking up the atmosphere and I was at home as soon as I walked out onto court. In the knock-up, I didn't miss a ball, I just felt so comfortable. It was extraordinary. Some courts you struggle with sighting the ball, some courts don't have good runback areas, but Centre Court has just the right dimensions, intimate yet spacious. It oozes class and I've enjoyed some special moments there.

The victory over Kafelnikov has a special place in my heart because it was the first opportunity to prove myself on the big stage and to make people remember me for my tennis. In 1995, I became the first player in 120 years to be disqualified from the tournament. I was frustrated and lashed out at a loose ball, which hit a ball-girl on the head. I apologized and, next day, bought her a bunch of flowers. But the incident taught me first about the excesses of the English tabloid media, and made me more determined than ever to make sure that it wasn't going to be the most vivid memory of my Wimbledon career. The funny thing now is that people recall the incident, know someone was disqualified, but don't remember it was me.

Thankfully, that has been replaced by some great memories. The victory over Kafelnikov in a match that had everything. I was two sets up, he came back to level, I saved two match points with aces and I found I thrived on the support of the crowd. The match against Richard Krajicek in 1997, was so close all the way and was interrupted overnight, but I still beat the defending champion and, though I didn't play at my best, the victory over

Tim Henman, 1998 (opposite)

PHOTOGRAPH BY ALEX LIVESEY

Paul Haarhuis on the Middle Sunday that same year was a unique occasion for me. You can draw on those memories every year now. If I go to Wimbledon in the off-season, I'll go up to Centre Court and have a quick look, just to check nothing has changed. It draws you in.

To me, there is no other tennis venue like Wimbledon. Just walking in through the gates is special. I'm not someone who is for tradition just for tradition's sake, but the traditions at Wimbledon mark it out from other tournaments and I think that's a general view in the locker-room, not just mine. The men's Champion defending his title at 2pm on the opening day; the bowing to the royal box, the grass itself. There aren't many grasscourt tournaments left now. The absence of sponsorship boards on Centre Court, the scheduling. To me, these are all traditions that help to make Wimbledon the most prestigious tournament in the world. It's certainly the focal point of my year and always will be. I've come close to winning, but have been unfortunate to meet Pete Sampras twice in the Semi-Finals. People ask if all the attention and the pressure gets me down. The answer is no. I'm exhausted at the end of Wimbledon, but I wouldn't want it to be any other way. I thrive on the atmosphere both on and off court and that will be the case until I stop coming to play.

Tim Henman, 1997 (left)
PHOTOGRAPH BY ROSS KINNAIRD

Ken McGregor, 1951 (left)
Sven Davidson, 1956 (top)
Lew Hoad, 1956 (above)

Anna Kournikova, 1997 (above left)

PHOTOGRAPH BY STU FORSTER

Venus Williams, 1998 (above right)

PHOTOGRAPH BY GARY M PRIOR

Jana Novotna, 1997 (opposite)

PHOTOGRAPH BY CLIVE BRUNSKILL

Mirjana Lucic, 1998 (above left)
Goran Ivanisevic, 1998 (above right)
Michael Chang, 1994 (opposite)
PHOTOGRAPHS BY GARY M PRIOR

Bjorn Borg, 1980 (above centre)
PHOTOGRAPH ALLSPORT HISTORICAL COLLECTION © HULTON GETTY

⁶At Wimbledon, every shot you hit counts

and if you don't put everything into every stroke

of every rally, there's a good chance

you're going to lose every point.⁹

Andre Agassi

1992 CHAMPION, ON LEARNING TO PLAY GRASSCOURT TENNIS.

Weather vane, 1999 (above left)

PHOTOGRAPH BY GARY M PRIOR

Serve (above right)

PHOTOGRAPH BY ANTON WANT

Jonas Bjorkman, 1995 (left)

PHOTOGRAPH BY MICHAEL COOPER

John McEnroe, 1979 (opposite)
PHOTOGRAPH ALLSPORT HISTORICAL COLLECTION
© HULTON GETTY

Snow on Number 1 Court, 1994 (right top)
PHOTOGRAPH BY MICHAEL COOPER

Fred Perry statue, 1991 (right centre)
PHOTOGRAPH BY RUSSELL CHEYNE

Umbrellas, 1997 (right bottom)
PHOTOGRAPH BY STU FORSTER

Play is suspended…

Rain stops play, 1985 (above)

PHOTOGRAPH BY STEVE POWELL

Umbrellas, undated (right)

PHOTOGRAPH ALLSPORT HISTORICAL COLLECTION © HULTON GETTY

Play is suspended...

Spectators in the rain, undated (above)

PHOTOGRAPH ALLSPORT HISTORICAL COLLECTION © HULTON GETTY

MY WIMBLEDON

by Chris Gorringe
Chief Executive, All England Club

At my interview for the job of Assistant Secretary, I was asked what I thought was a rather strange question. 'Mr Gorringe, would you expect to stay here for the rest of your life?' I was twenty-seven at the time and I replied politely that if they enjoyed having me and I enjoyed it, Wimbledon was the sort of place you might contemplate staying for a long time. Twenty-six years on, I am still here. I never expected to stay so long, but, in all honesty, I cannot think of anywhere else I would rather work.

The joy of working here is that you are involved in something you really believe in, working in a nice environment with nice people and, for two weeks every year, the eyes of the sporting world focus on what for the other fifty weeks is a private members' tennis club. At 10.30am on the first Monday of The Championships, the gates open and a wave of fans flow through and, for a moment you think: 'What are all these people doing here?' But it's a wonderful sight, exhilarating and nerve-racking at the same time. The Championships are here again and all the work that has been put in through the year, all the big decisions and the small decisions we've taken, will be judged over the next Fortnight. It's a love-hate relationship during the Fortnight, like preparing for a big exam every year.

I always think of my predecessor, Tony Cooper, who once woke up in a cold sweat on the night before The Championships when he realized he hadn't ordered the tennis balls. 'Oh my God,' he thought. 'We've got a tennis championships and no tennis balls.' He needn't have worried, of course. Slazenger have been providing tennis balls for The Championships since 1902 and were not about to forget. There is a natural rhythm to the preparation, but we are always looking to improve. You can see that by the changing skyline, the new Number 1 Court and the new media centre. The day we say: 'Well, we can't do any better than that' is the day Wimbledon's reputation starts to decline.

The worst job I have, the one I dread the most, is relaying news of rain delays or abandonments over the PA system. I hate public speaking anyway, but it is so important to communicate with the fans and I feel that if I'm doing it, I'm in control, even if I make a mess of it. My heart sinks when I look out of the window and the skies are grey or it's raining. I feel sorry for everyone, for the fans, for the staff, for the players. But you just have to get on with it. The perfect fortnight is when I can forget about the loudspeaker completely.

My own memories are bound up in Wimbledon as a Club as well as The Championships. There is no more spectacular view of the clubhouse than in the autumn when the creeper turns red and the evening sun slants across it. The first time anyone walks out

to play on the grasscourts in May, that's an evocative time, especially if you're lucky enough to do it yourself. I've played on Centre Court twenty-five years out of the last twenty-six. The Chairman of the Club usually invites the Club Committee and the senior executives to play on Centre and Number 1 Court the week after The Championships.

You are always conscious of the progression of the seasons and always aware that the turn of a new month brings you closer to the next Championships.

The garden of my house overlooks the practice courts at Aorangi Park and, once, Martina Navratilova stopped by for tea after a practice session. Another day, my two girls had been watching Steffi Graf practise and when she finished her session she invited them onto the court to play. She hadn't a clue who they were, but it was a nice touch. You get to know some players better than others. Whether they like it or not, the Champions become part of us and we become part of them.

Andre Agassi paid us a surprise visit the November after he'd won the title, in 1992, and had lunch in the Members' Dining Room upstairs. He happened to see the club's Christmas card, which had a picture of him on the front, and ordered 100 on the spot.

I recall when I became Secretary of the Club in 1980 just walking onto the Centre Court on Finals day, with the table out and the trophy there, and seeing the Centre Court absolutely full. It's a thrill every time and I love listening to the band on Centre Court before play on Finals weekend. I watched from the back of the Committee Box when Virginia Wade won The Centenary Championships. The opening of the new Number 1 Court, in 1997, was a memorable occasion with the parade of Champions. Wimbledon has been a big part of my life. But, when I've retired, I will come back and watch some tennis rather than sitting in my office watching it on a small television screen and praying it doesn't rain.

Rain over Wimbledon, 1997
PHOTOGRAPH BY CLIVE BRUNSKILL

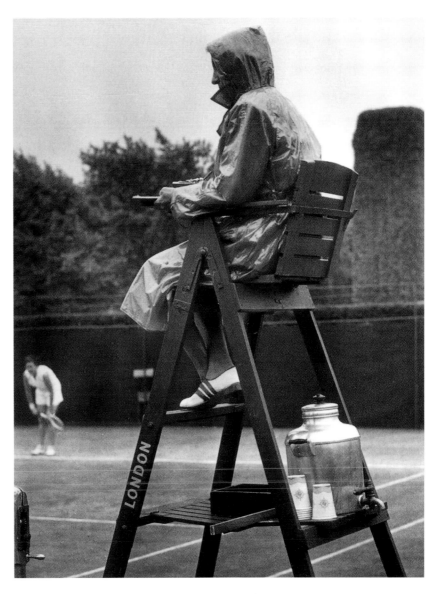

(Clockwise from top left)

Champagne in the rain, 1999

PHOTOGRAPH BY CLIVE BRUNSKILL

Tennis in the rain, 1947

Spectators in the rain, 1980

PHOTOGRAPH ALLSPORT HISTORICAL COLLECTION
© HULTON GETTY

≈ The Photograph Shows ≈
1947

A damp job at Wimbledon.
The Ladies Plate match (above) between Miss De Borman of Belgium and
Miss E M Wilford of Great Britain was played in pouring rain throughout at
Wimbledon today. The umpire had an unpleasant job,
but she was well clad to cope with the weather.

≈

Play is suspended…

Gates in the rain, 1997 (top)
PHOTOGRAPH BY GARY M PRIOR

Players waiting for the rain to stop, 1950 (above)
PHOTOGRAPH ALLSPORT HISTORICAL COLLECTION © HULTON GETTY

Rainbow over Wimbledon, 1998 (right)
PHOTOGRAPH BY MIKE HEWITT

Play is suspended..

(Clockwise from top left) *Spectators, 1993*

PHOTOGRAPH BY CHRIS COLE

Line judge, 1994

PHOTOGRAPH BY GARY M PRIOR

Spectators, 1990

PHOTOGRAPH BY BOB MARTIN

Anna Kournikova, 1999

PHOTOGRAPH BY ALEX LIVESEY

Mirjana Lucic, 1999 (opposite)

PHOTOGRAPH BY GARY M PRIOR

MY WIMBLEDON

by Stefan Edberg
Wimbledon Champion 1988, 1990

I grew up watching two tournaments on Swedish television: one was the Davis Cup and the other was Wimbledon, so when I first played there it was like a dream. I stayed in a hotel in Richmond alone, and took the bus to Wimbledon Village, changing at Kingston. When I got there, I couldn't see the courts and had to ask someone where they were. That was 1983 and as well as playing the junior tournament I was the last player into the senior draw.

I beat Boris [Becker] in the first round of the juniors – I can't remember which court it was exactly, 9 or 10, somewhere out in the wilds. I lost 8-6 in the fifth to Henrik Sundstrom in the second round of the senior competition. We played for hours and hours on Court 6. I was heartbroken because the winner was due to play Jimmy Connors in the next round and I really wanted that experience. I knew I'd be back but when you're young you don't think like that. The following week, I beat John Frawley in the final of the juniors on Number 1 Court. We started at the same time as John McEnroe and Chris Lewis in the Final on Centre Court and the cheers echoed across the court from next door. I think we finished at the same time

too, because McEnroe won pretty easily.

Playing at Wimbledon for the first time is huge for a young player. You hear so much about how many rules there are, what you can do and what you can't do and sometimes you wonder why you have to do this and do that. But it all comes with the tradition of the place and the more you come back the more you appreciate that it's part of Wimbledon. The post is always in the same place, the faces are the same, the rituals stay the same. It is like a familiar old overcoat. You instantly feel comfortable inside it.

For me, coming onto Centre Court as defending Champion at 2pm on the first Monday of the tournament was one of the greatest feelings in the game. It was like a boxing match; people are talking quietly and then some of them can see the players walking out through the doors and the applause begins to roll around the court until it erupts when the players step onto the court. On Centre Court, you have both extremes. When a match is really tight, you can hear a pin drop. But it can also be alive and kicking. The crowd really know the game and show respect to the players. It's also a big court, yet can feel pretty intimate as the crowd is so close. I always

Stefan Edberg, 1989 (opposite)

PHOTOGRAPH BY BOB MARTIN

Play is suspended...

Stefan Edberg, 1990 (above)
Stefan Edberg, 1991 (opposite)

PHOTOGRAPHS BY ALLSPORT

wanted to play there. It gave me such an advantage.

From the time I moved up to the locker-room for the top seeds, I always used the same locker. After a while, if you were there long enough, the dressing-room attendant would make sure you kept it. 'This is reserved for Mr Becker', 'this is reserved for Mr Edberg.' I had one in the corner, number twenty-one. Boris, strangely, was in the same section, number seven, I think, which meant that when we played our three finals we were never far away from each other. The attendant would ask whether you wanted towels when your match was called onto court, then it was out up the stairs, past the honours boards in the hall and through the doors into the little room beneath the stand where you waited to go out.

Three years in a row, Boris and I went through that routine before the Final. He crushed me once and I won the other two. We were about the same age, both good grasscourt players and our rivalry went back a long way. We were always looking over our shoulders at each other. He won Wimbledon at seventeen and that made me believe I could do it and so it went on throughout our careers. Boris was a great competitor. He could lose to some guys he should have beaten but for the big occasion, he was always ready. If we played now, we would both want to win just as much.

In 1988, we only played a few games on the Sunday because of rain. I broke and he broke back in the last game before rain. I worried all night about it, but I won in four sets the next day. If I close my eyes now, I can remember the weather, the feeling, everything about that moment because it's the first time, which is always special. The 1990 Final was a closer match. I played great tennis for a couple of sets, he came back to level and had an easy forehand volley at 3-1 in the fifth, which he missed. It was just a little mistake, but critical. I remember the backhand lob that got me the vital break. I was on the back foot and instinctively flicked my wrist at the ball and the lob fell in. Those are the sort of shots and points you remember. Equally, I can recall starting a first-round match on Centre Court with Marc Rosset on Monday afternoon and not finishing it until Thursday. I had to spend every day from 9am until 6pm wandering from the changing-room to the restaurant and back because there was just nowhere else to go. But that is all part of Wimbledon too.

Change ends, please...

(Opposite, clockwise
from top left)
Spectator, 1995
PHOTOGRAPH BY GARY M PRIOR

Goran Ivanisevic, 1998
PHOTOGRAPH BY ALEX LIVESEY

Yannick Noah, 1987
PHOTOGRAPH BY RUSSELL CHEYNE

Venus Williams, 1997
PHOTOGRAPH BY CLIVE BRUNSKILL

Anna Kournikova, 1997 (right
above)
PHOTOGRAPH BY STU FORSTER

Streaker, 1996 (right below)
PHOTOGRAPH BY GARY M PRIOR

John McEnroe, 1992
('Change ends, please...', pages
12-13)
PHOTOGRAPH BY CHRIS COLE

Change ends, please...

Boris Becker, 1989 (above)

PHOTOGRAPH BY SIMON BRUTY

The crush for a view on Court 14, 1976 (right)

PHOTOGRAPH ALLSPORT HISTORICAL COLLECTION © HULTON GETTY

‘This is where I was born, in 1985.’

BORIS BECKER

ON THE CENTRE COURT.

Change ends, please...

Tea on the lawns at Worple Road, 1906

Visions of Wimbledon

Strawberry girl, 1995 (top left)

PHOTOGRAPH BY MICHAEL COOPER

Pimms, 1997 (top right)

Andre Agassi, 1995 (above)

PHOTOGRAPHS BY CLIVE BRUNSKILL

Change ends, please...

Strawberries, 1994 (left)

(Above, clockwise from top left)
Greg Rusedski, 1996
Marcelo Rios, 1995
Stefan Edberg, 1993
Leonardo Lavalle, 1992

Change ends, please...

Match Point

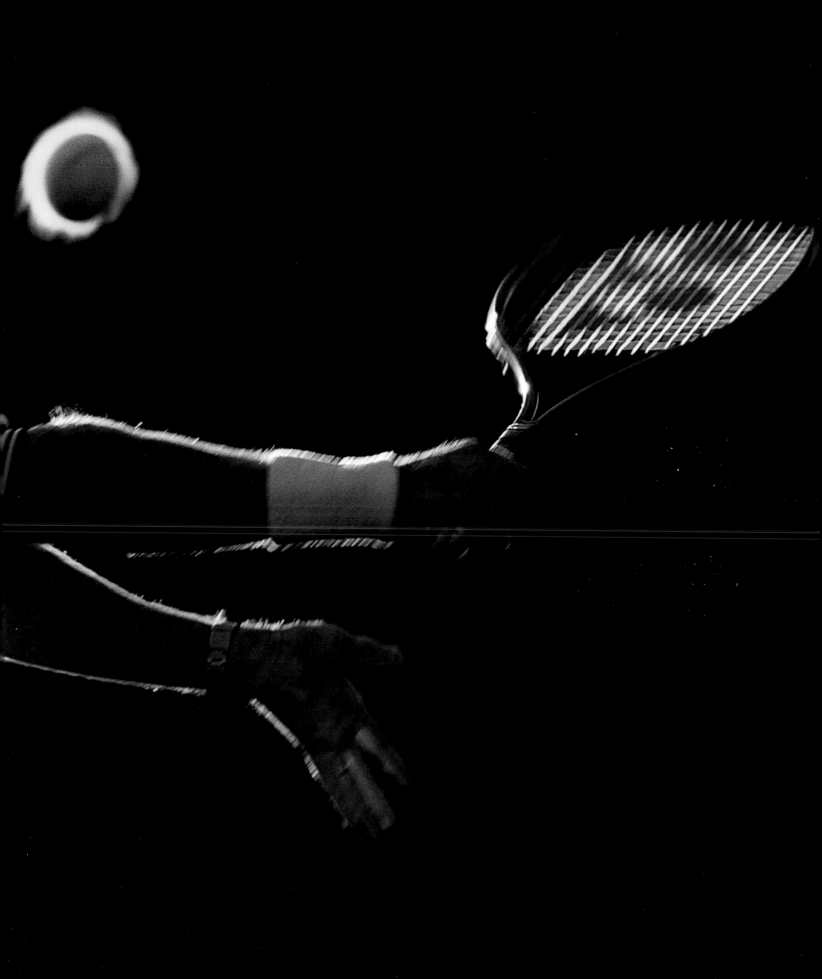

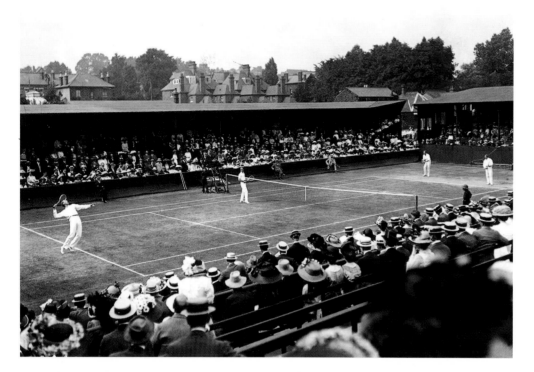

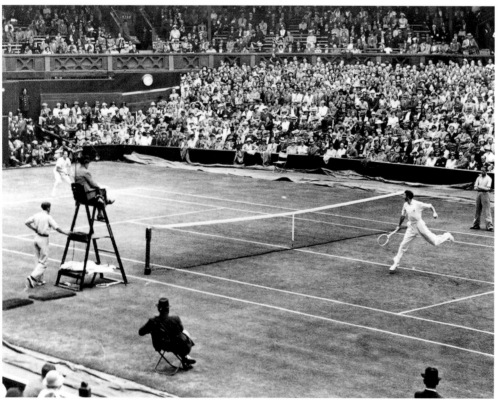

Men's doubles, 1911
(left above)
PHOTOGRAPH ALLSPORT HISTORICAL
COLLECTION © HULTON GETTY

*Gottfried Von Cramm
playing Don Budge, 1937*
(left below)
PHOTOGRAPH WIMBLEDON
LAWN TENNIS MUSEUM

Wimbledon crowds, 1990
(right)
PHOTOGRAPH BY DAN SMITH

Todd Woodbridge, 1998
('Match Point', pages 78-9)
PHOTOGRAPH BY ALEX LIVESEY

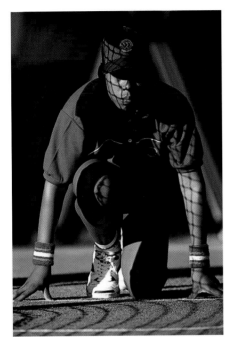

Bjorn Borg, 1980 (opposite)
PHOTOGRAPH BY STEVE POWELL

Ball-boys and ball-girls in action (top)
PHOTOGRAPHS BY CLIVE BRUNSKILL

Andre Agassi, 1991 (above)
PHOTOGRAPH BY BOB MARTIN

Match Point

❛Winning Wimbledon means, well, I guess it means everything really.

This is what I've been working for, for many, many, years.

This is a definite dream come true for me.❜

JANA NOVOTNA,

1998 CHAMPION.

Jana Novotna, 1997 (opposite)

PHOTOGRAPH BY GARY M PRIOR

Jennifer Capriati, 1998 (above)

PHOTOGRAPH BY MIKE HEWITT

Match Point

Virginia Wade, 1977 (above left)

PHOTOGRAPH BY TONY DUFFY

Ann Jones, 1969 (above right)
Billie-Jean King, 1968 (right)

PHOTOGRAPHS ALLSPORT HISTORICAL COLLECTION © HULTON GETTY

❛This is where my heart is, no matter where in the world I am.

I know and love every inch of that court.

It's my place.❜

BILLE JEAN KING

ON CENTRE COURT.

Visions of Wimbledon

Match Point

Andre Agassi, 1998 (top)

PHOTOGRAPH BY MIKE HEWITT

Tim Henman, 1998 (above)

PHOTOGRAPH BY GARY M PRIOR

Ivan Lendl, 1981 (left)

PHOTOGRAPH BY ALLSPORT

(Above, clockwise from top left)
Helen Wills Moody, 1933 and Kitty Godfree, 1924
PHOTOGRAPHS WIMBLEDON LAWN TENNIS MUSEUM

Jean Borotra, 1935 and Fred Perry, 1936
PHOTOGRAPHS ALLSPORT HISTORICAL COLLECTION © HULTON GETTY

Suzanne Lenglen, 1924 (right)
PHOTOGRAPH ALLSPORT HISTORICAL COLLECTION © HULTON GETTY

Visions of Wimbledon

Match Point

A Viera, 1954 (opposite)

PHOTOGRAPH ALLSPORT HISTORICAL COLLECTION © HULTON GETTY

Boris Becker, 1988 (above left)

PHOTOGRAPH BY BOB MARTIN

Anke Huber, 1995 (above centre)

PHOTOGRAPH BY GARY M PRIOR

Andre Agassi, 1992 (above right)

PHOTOGRAPH BY CHRIS COLE

Jim Courier, losing to Guy Forget, 1994 (above)

PHOTOGRAPH BY GARY M PRIOR

John McEnroe, losing to Bjorn Borg, 1980 (left)

PHOTOGRAPH ALLSPORT HISTORICAL COLLECTION © HULTON GETTY

Match Point

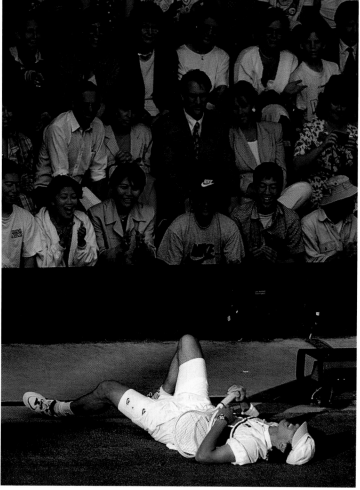

Martina Navratilova, 1987
(left above)

PHOTOGRAPH BY ALLSPORT

Cedric Pioline, 1995 (left below)

PHOTOGRAPH BY CLIVE MASON

David Wheaton, 1991 (opposite
above)

PHOTOGRAPH BY RUSSELL CHEYNE

Alex Metreveli, 1973 (opposite
below)

PHOTOGRAPH ALLSPORT HISTORICAL COLLECTION
© HULTON GETTY

Match Point

Gabriela Sabatini (above)

PHOTOGRAPH BY CLIVE BRUNSKILL

Arantxa Sanchez Vicario, 1996 (top)
PHOTOGRAPH BY CLIVE BRUNSKILL

Virginia Wade, 1983 (above)
PHOTOGRAPH BY DAVID CANNON

Match Point

Jean Forbes, the sixteen-year-old South African player who fell during her Centre Court match (right) with Louise Brough, is seen in this picture showing her injured knee to the match referee on Centre Court. The injury caused Miss Forbes to break into tears.

Gigi Fernandez, 1994 (above left)
PHOTOGRAPH BY CLIVE BRUNSKILL

Conchita Martinez, 1995 (above right)
PHOTOGRAPH BY ALLSPORT

Jean Forbes, 1956 (right)

Match Point

Ilie Nastase, 1980 (above)
Ilie Nastase signing autographs, 1973 (opposite)

(Opposite, clockwise
from top left)
John McEnroe, 1980
PHOTOGRAPH ALLSPORT HISTORICAL
COLLECTION © HULTON GETTY

Arantxa Sanchez Vicario, 1997
PHOTOGRAPH BY STU FORSTER

John McEnroe, 1991
PHOTOGRAPH BY SIMON BRUTY

Ilie Nastase, 1980
PHOTOGRAPH ALLSPORT HISTORICAL
COLLECTION © HULTON GETTY

John McEnroe, 1980
PHOTOGRAPH BY STEVE POWELL

Ilie Nastase, 1977 (right)
PHOTOGRAPH ALLSPORT HISTORICAL
COLLECTION © HULTON GETTY

≈ The Photograph Shows ≈
1977

Nastase is booed off court after umpire storm.
During his match against Andrew Pattison, of Rhodesia, Ilie Nastase (above) was near defeat in the fourth set when
he upset Pattison's concentration by holding up play for ten minutes after demanding referee Fred Hoyles come to
the court because he wanted more linesmen. At that stage, Nastase was two sets down and 5–3 down in the fourth.
After the interruption he went on to win the fourth set, and then won the match by taking the final set.

≈

Jimmy Connors, 1988 (above left)

PHOTOGRAPH BY BOB MARTIN

Boris Becker, 1995 (above right)

PHOTOGRAPH BY CLIVE BRUNSKILL

Greg Rusedski, 1995 (opposite)

PHOTOGRAPH BY GARY M PRIOR

MY WIMBLEDON

by Rod Laver
Wimbledon Champion 1961, 1962, 1968, 1969.

When I was growing up in Australia, I would listen to some of the older players talking about Wimbledon. So I had an idea of what a big event it was. I remember staying at Lew Hoad's place once and seeing the trophies he'd won at Wimbledon. But not until I got there myself did I realize quite how big it is. It beat every expectation I'd ever had. I played my first match there when I was seventeen. I had to qualify at Roehampton and the mere fact of playing at Wimbledon was part of a young boy's dreams – at the time it was the crowning moment of a career. Everyone in the world played at Wimbledon.

Wimbledon can overwhelm players, particularly young ones. It either heightens your concentration and you play well, or you crumble. Concentration was not my strong point early in my career but at Wimbledon I could lift my levels of concentration because of the surroundings and because I knew how important it was. Then the dreams start to change a bit. Instead of dreaming of playing at Wimbledon, you dream of reaching the Final, then you dream of winning the whole damn thing.

For me, winning the title was a case of third time lucky. It was a big surprise that I was in the Final in 1959. I played Alex Olmedo and, quite simply, he was better than I was. He was unbelievably talented, very quick and grass was his best surface. In only my third Wimbledon, I felt fortunate just to be in the Final and so hoped rather than expected to win. I was unseeded and he was the number one seed. But I learnt from the experience, which is half the battle at Wimbledon, and I became a better competitor. I liked the rituals of Wimbledon, finding out your draw, looking at the papers in the morning

Rod Laver, 1968 (opposite)

≈ The Photograph Shows ≈
1968

The champ is at full stretch.
Australian Rod Laver, ranked World No 1 and top seed, is for a moment put at full stretch during his men's singles final game against fellow-countryman Tony Roche on Centre Court. Laver was put under pressure at only brief moments during the match that he won quite easily in three straight sets.

≈

Match Point

*Princess Marina presents Rod Laver with the Men's Singles
Championship Cup, 1961* (above)

Visions of Wimbledon

to see what court you're on and when. When I was playing on Centre Court, I enjoyed getting into the little annexe below the stand before the match; it gave me a chance to visualize how the match might go. I felt like I could handle the daunting experience of Centre Court better than my opponent.

In my second final, I met my countryman Neale Fraser, a tall leftie with a lethal kicking serve and I lost a very tight match. But both those defeats prepared me for the day I won my first title, against Chuck McKinley, and for defending the title the following year against Martin Mulligan. To be honest, it is hard to recall much about those days. My philosophy was always to win and get off court as quickly as possible, then read about your victory in the press later. Each victory was important for different reasons. Beating Tony Roche in the 1968 Final was good for the professionals, who had just been allowed to play again at Wimbledon, as well as for me. When I turned professional in 1963, I

thought sacrificing Wimbledon was one of the prices I had to pay. I never thought I would have the chance to come back.

I can recall one particular moment in the 1969 Final with John Newcombe. He had levelled the match at 1-1 in sets and I was 4-1 down in the third. He served and pushed the volley into my backhand. We knew each other's games pretty well and I knew he would expect me to go down the line. Instead, I clipped it back across court in front of him and he muttered: 'Goddam it'. I felt that the tide began to turn at that moment and I won in four sets, the third leg of the Grand Slam. Those were just the little subtleties of playing on grass. Break point down, second serve, hit the ball a little faster and wider. Tricks of the trade, if you like.

I come back to Wimbledon when I can, depending on my schedule and my health. I still get the same feeling walking in through the Church Road gates. I'm here, it's old home week again.

John Newcombe, 1969 (above)

Match Point

Fred Perry statue, 1999 (above)

PHOTOGRAPH BY ALEX LIVESEY

Fred Perry v Frank Shields, Davis Cup, 1934 (right)

PHOTOGRAPH ALLSPORT HISTORICAL COLLECTION © HULTON GETTY

Match Point

≈ The Photograph Shows ≈
1955

The Danny Kaye of the contest.
A Huber of Austria – known as the 'Danny Kaye of Wimbledon' –
continues his antics by 'flying' for a ball – during his match
with G L Ward of Great Britain, at Wimbledon today.

≈

Cedric Pioline, 1997 (left)
PHOTOGRAPH BY CLIVE BRUNSKILL

A Huber, 1955 (above)
PHOTOGRAPH ALLSPORT HISTORICAL COLLECTION © HULTON GETTY

Match Point

The only way to break Boris Becker on grass is if he hits two double faults, you hit a lucky return and at 0–40 he falls down accidentally before he hits the volley.

MIKAEL PERNFORS
SWEDISH DAVIS CUP PLAYER,
ON PLAYING BORIS BECKER
AT WIMBLEDON.

He's the Michael Jordan of Germany.

PETE SAMPRAS
ON BECKER.

Boris Becker, 1993
PHOTOGRAPH BY CHRIS COLE

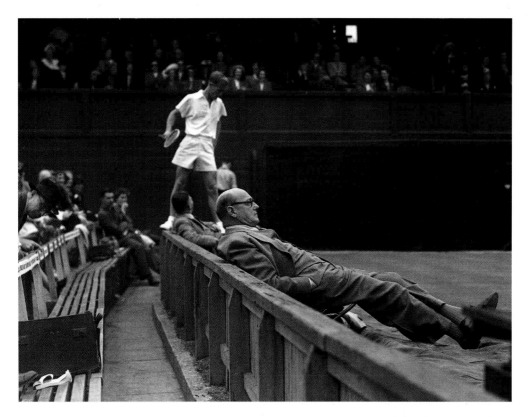

≈ The Photograph Shows ≈
1947

Out of Court!
The All-England Lawn Tennis Club's 1947 Championships began at Wimbledon, London today, and a galaxy of stars began a week-long struggle for the world's premier title. O W Sidwell (Australia), chasing a wide ball, (left) couldn't stop and jumped the barrier around Number 1 Court during his five set match against B Patty (USA). The gentleman reclining in the foreground is not resting – he's a line judge!

≈

OW Sidwell, 1947, (left)
PHOTOGRAPH ALLSPORT HISTORICAL COLLECTION © HULTON GETTY

Jim Courier, 1993 (above left)
PHOTOGRAPHS BY BOB MARTIN

Bunny Austin, 1936 (above right)
PHOTOGRAPH ALLSPORT HISTORICAL COLLECTION © HULTON GETTY

Visions of Wimbledon

M J Anderson, 1956
(right above)
Arthur Ashe, 1970,
(right below)

MY WIMBLEDON

by Martina Navratilova
Nine-times Wimbledon Champion

There are so many memories of Wimbledon, it is almost like a sequence in a dream. When I left the Centre Court for the last time, I picked up a piece of grass because that court, in particular, had been a part of my life for more than twenty years. The funny thing was that my first match on Centre Court was an accident. It was 1974 and it was a first-round match against Mima Jausovec. We had no right to be anywhere near Centre Court, but scheduled play had finished for the day on Centre and so they asked us to play there. This was only my second year at the tournament. We split sets, but it started raining at 2-2 in the third and we didn't get back on that night. By rights, in the morning, we should have been second on Centre to finish, but they sent us off to Court 3 and I ended up losing in fifteen minutes.

That was my second year. My first experience of Wimbledon, in 1973, was a bit bewildering. I had wanted to enter Queen's, but my entry form had been posted from Rome and the Italian post was on strike, so it never arrived. So Wimbledon was my first ever grasscourt tournament. I was in the bottom dressing-room where all the lower ranked players

change, it rained like crazy and I played backgammon with Chris Evert and Rosie Casals. I remember playing mixed doubles against Billie Jean King and wondering: 'Where on earth did she come from?' Strangely, when I came back in 1974, I went to the bottom dressing-room, no sign of my name. Went upstairs, no sign of my name there either and eventually found that I was with the big names in the lady members' dressing-room. I still have no idea why, but I felt a bit uncomfortable because I hadn't earned the privilege.

Even back then, I knew the Centre Court was ideal for my style of game. Because of the green awnings at the back of the court and because the crowd at either end is seated relatively high in the stand, you never lose the ball, which is critical for a serve and volleyer. If you lose on Centre Court, there are no excuses. You lost because you weren't good enough on the day. The grass, which is a fast surface, obviously suited the way I played, but there is an aura about Centre Court which is unique. It is the silence, the complete absence of sound. You can hear everything that happens around the court. On

Martina Navratilova, 1987 (left)

PHOTOGRAPH BY CHRIS COLE

other courts, there is always a buzz. Centre Court is like a theatre and a magical play is being staged and you can hear the actors breathing. Shut my eyes now and I can still feel that silence. I had so many special times on that court, mostly good, a few bad.

There are strange moments like 1976 when I was foot-faulted at 1-1 in the third set in the semi-finals. I've never been foot-faulted in my life because I stood three inches behind the baseline to serve. I knew the linesman and so I just turned and shouted at him: 'What are you doing?' I lost the match. My first Final when I beat Chris (Evert), she was very sweet and very happy for me. I think we both knew there would be many other times. But my last Final against Chris, in 1985, ended controversially and quite bitterly. Chris's final passing shot clipped the net and was narrowly out. I wheeled round and looked at the linesman, who belatedly put his arm out to make the call. Chris thought the ball was in and had turned back to serve again, so when she heard 'Game, set and match to Navratilova' she was upset. It was a disappointing way to end a great rivalry.

Beating Hana (Mandlikova) the following year was perhaps my most difficult Final. I was down 5-2 and won 7-5 6-3, but there was the whole 'Czech thing' between us. Her father knew my mother and she always gave me fits because she was so unpredictable. With Chris, I knew her game so well, there was nothing we could do to surprise each other. Hana was completely different. And then there was the record-breaking ninth title, against Zina Garrison, which looked an easy victory on paper but was tough mentally. I had worked so hard for the record and had been playing in pain for so long, it was just a relief to get that title.

I know Wimbledon inside out. It's like my home. I remember my sister came back to Wimbledon ten years after her first visit and found the same guy on the same gate. There was always that sense of familiarity and tradition. Same times, same places, same faces. Professionals like that sort of routine. I sometimes wished I could walk around the place without being recognized. I only went to the Museum for the first time recently. Sometimes, late in the evenings before the tournament, I would go and sit on the empty Centre Court, just to feel the place again. I'll do it even now. I feel part of the tapestry.

Martina Navratilova, 1991 (right above)
PHOTOGRAPH BY BOB MARTIN

Martina Navratilova and Conchita Martinez, 1994 (right below)
PHOTOGRAPH BY CLIVE BRUNSKILL

❛Just about everyday I think about tennis and tennis, for me, is Wimbledon.❜

MARTINA NAVRATILOVA.

I never realised what it all meant. Nothing, and I mean nothing, compares with winning Wimbledon.

ANDRE AGASSI

(Opposite, clockwise from top left)
Bjorn Borg, 1979
PHOTOGRAPH BY TONY DUFFY

Andre Agassi, 1992
PHOTOGRAPH BY BOB MARTIN

Goran Ivanisevic, 1998
PHOTOGRAPH BY GARY M PRIOR

Boris Becker, 1985
Henri Leconte, 1987
PHOTOGRAPHS BY ALLSPORT

Pete Sampras, 1999
PHOTOGRAPH BY GARY M PRIOR

Steffi Graf, 1995 (right)
PHOTOGRAPH BY GARY M PRIOR

It's been great. I have to say it's been great here.

STEFFI GRAF

❛I walked to my chair after he told me, kind of stunned. Wimbledon and Boris went together. I mean, this is where he made his mark as a seventeen−year−old and it was like his living room out there on Centre Court.

He'll be missed by the fans and the tournament. He was a class act on and off court.❜

PETE SAMPRAS
REFLECTING ON HIS DEFEAT OF BECKER IN 1998.
AT THE END OF THE MATCH, BECKER TOLD SAMPRAS IT WAS HIS
LAST MATCH AT WIMBLEDON. BECKER PLAYED AGAIN IN 1999
BEFORE FINALLY RETIRING.

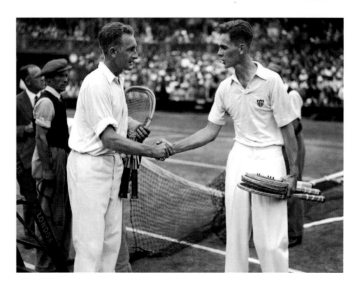

Fred Perry victorious, 1935
(left top)
Jack Crawford and Elsworth Vines, 1933
(left below)
PHOTOGRAPHS ALLSPORT HISTORICAL COLLECTION
© HULTON GETTY

Pete Sampras and Boris Becker, 1997
(left centre)
PHOTOGRAPH BY ROSS KINNAIRD

6There's an electricity out there, which lets you go through games and whole sets without realizing what's happening.9

JOHN NEWCOMBE
THREE TIMES WIMBLEDON CHAMPION,
ON THE ATMOSPHERE OF
CENTRE COURT.

John Newcombe, 1967
PHOTOGRAPH ALLSPORT HISTORICAL
COLLECTION © HULTON GETTY

≈ The Photograph Shows ≈
1967

John Newcombe of Australia defeated Wilhelm Bungert of Germany on the Centre
Court at Wimbledon to win the world's premier tennis title. The spring-heeled
Champion leaps the net after beating Bungert in three sets.

≈

Game, Set, Championship

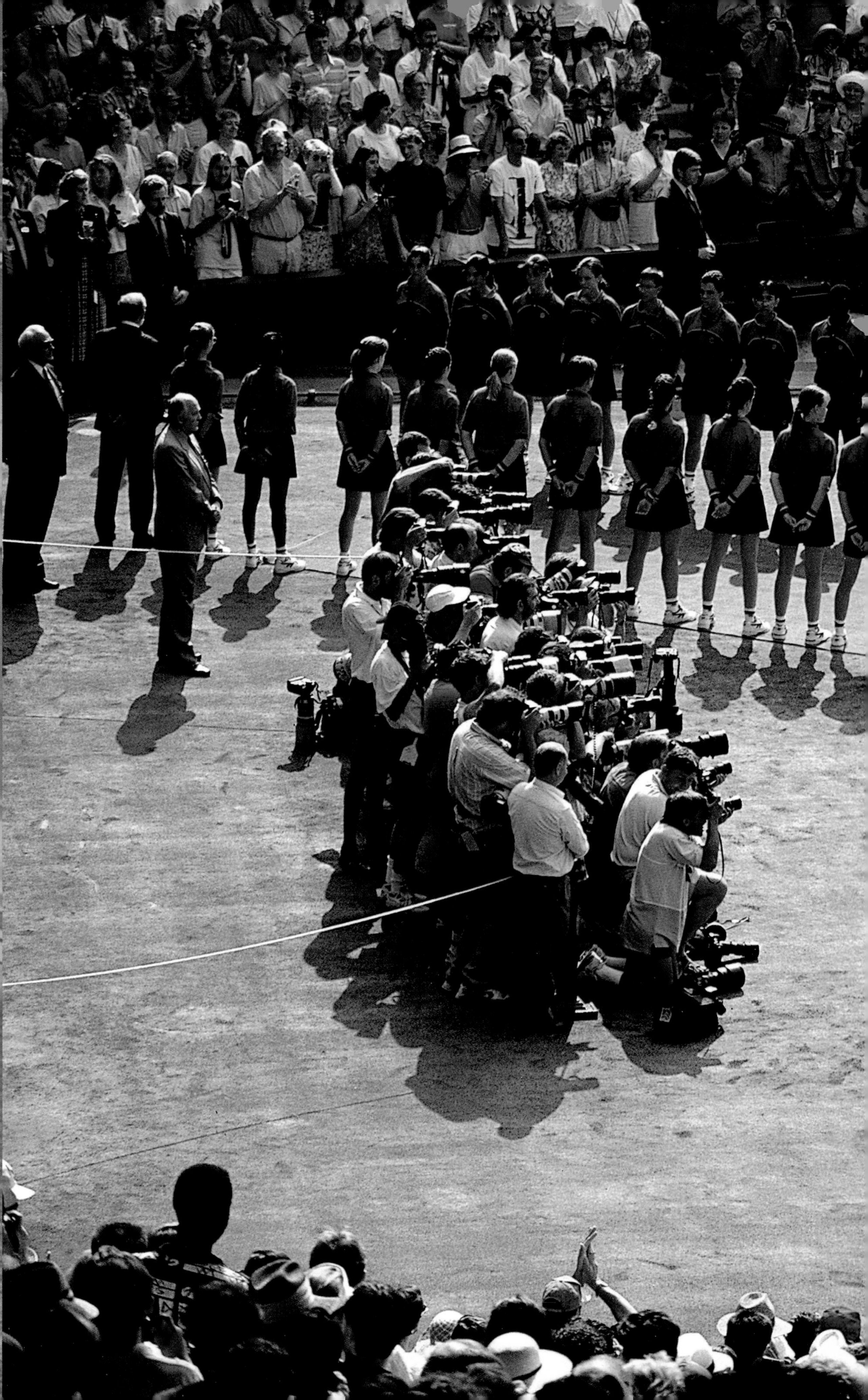

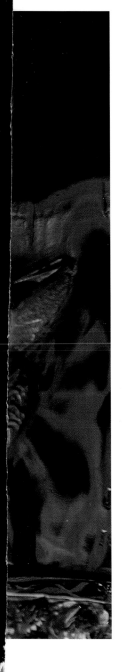

‘I was fortunate enough to play against McEnroe, Connors, Lendl, even Borg a little bit, but he is the most complete player. He has the power, the speed, the touch and though you can't compare the sixties to the nineties I always felt that he was the best player ever.’

BORIS BECKER
ON PETE SAMPRAS, SIX TIMES CHAMPION.

1995 Men's Singles trophy (left)
PHOTOGRAPH BY GARY M PRIOR

Pete Sampras' name is engraved on the 1997 trophy (right)
PHOTOGRAPH BY GARY M PRIOR

Pete Sampras, 1995
('Game, Set, Championship'
pages128-9)
PHOTOGRAPH BY CLIVE MASON

Game, Set, Championship

Dennis Ralston, defeated, 1966 (left)

Princess Margaret congratulates Jack Kramer, with King George VI and Queen Elizabeth in the Royal Box, 1947 (below left)

Jan Kodes, 1973 (right)

PHOTOGRAPHS ALLSPORT HISTORICAL COLLECTION © HULTON GETTY

❝Wimbledon is a bona fide, certified British tradition and British traditions are just a bit more traditional than anybody else's – just as British royalty is a bit more royal.❞

ARTHUR ASHE
(PORTRAIT IN MOTION, 1975)

Game, Set, Championship

Jana Novotna being consoled by the Duchess of Kent, 1993 (top)

PHOTOGRAPH BY CHRIS COLE

Billie Jean King and Princess Marina, Dutchess of Kent, 1968 (above)

*Mrs Leslie A (Kitty) Godfree being presented
with a medal by the Queen, 1926* (right)

PHOTOGRAPHS ALLSPORT HISTORICAL COLLECTION © HULTON GETTY

Game, Set, Championship

Martina Navratilova and Conchita Martinez, 1994 (opposite, top left)
Martina Hingis and Jana Novotna, 1997 (opposite, top right)
Arantxa Sanchez Vicario and Steffi Graf, 1995 (opposite, bottom left)
PHOTOGRAPHS BY CLIVE BRUNSKILL

Arantxa Sanchez Vicario and Steffi Graf, 1996 (opposite, bottom right)
PHOTOGRAPH BY STU FORSTER

Arantxa Sanchez Vicario and Steffi Graf, 1996 (above)
PHOTOGRAPH BY CLIVE BRUNSKILL

Game, Set, Championship

Roy Emerson and Fred Stolle, 1965

PHOTOGRAPH ALLSPORT HISTORICAL COLLECTION © HULTON GETTY

Visions of Wimbledon

MY WIMBLEDON

by Roy Emerson
Wimbledon Champion 1964, 1965

I played Willie Alvarez at Wimbledon, in 1959, and broke his serve in the opening game. He was a good clay court player, but not much of a grass-courter. I served four straight double-faults to lose my opening service game. I broke him again but served two more doubles to make it six in a row. I'd never done that before and have never done it since. I was seeded number eight that year and all I could think about was the people watching on television thinking: 'How the hell did this guy get to be seeded number eight?' Wimbledon can do that to you.

To me, Wimbledon is the Rolls Royce of tournaments. It has a little bit of mystique, a little bit of class. Way back in those amateur days, it was the one tournament where they went out of their way to look after the players and it was the one tournament that was televised. We didn't have television in the Queensland outback back then, but I can remember running to the store for batteries for my radio so that I could listen in the middle of the night.

Once I travelled as part of an Australian Davis Cup team and had all my expenses paid for me. Mostly, I've had to share rooms or rent a house with some of the other Australians. The most I ever got was £250, which was allocated as expenses for the tournament. But we had a good time and we enjoyed Wimbledon. We enjoyed the atmosphere and we loved playing on grass.

Wimbledon was not my luckiest tournament. Twice, injuries during the tournament cost me the chance of a title. In 1962, I was seeded second to Rod Laver, but I injured my toe during a doubles match on Number 1 Court on the first Saturday. Despite extensive treatment over the weekend and pain-killing injections before the match I had to retire at 1-1 in sets in my singles against Martin Mulligan, who went on to reach the Final. Four years later, when I was top seed, I dislocated my shoulder in the quarter-final against Owen Davidson. Nowadays, you would be allowed to have treatment on court, but there was no such luxury then. I played on, but could hardly throw the ball up to serve and, having already won the first set, lost the next three. People often commented on the strange wind-up in my service action. I had a pretty poor serve early in my career and I did a lot of work on it. Like a golfer on the putting green, I just found a method that seemed to work and it wasn't until one time at Wimbledon when I saw it on television that I realized how awful it looked. I had to go into the next room. But it did me OK.

The two titles I won, I beat Fred (Stolle) both times. The first Final, in 1964, I think it was, we had to come off the court four or five times because of rain and, in those days, you weren't allowed to warm up again when you came back on court. If you were serving 30-40, break point down, when you came off, you had to serve cold straight off as soon as play began again. They only had covers for two courts. Wimbledon has come a long way since then, but it was the best tournament then and it's still the best tournament now.

Pete Sampras, 1995 (left)

PHOTOGRAPH BY CLIVE BRUNSKILL

John McEnroe, 1983 (right above)

PHOTOGRAPH BY DAVID CANNON

Richard Krajicek, 1996 (right below)

PHOTOGRAPH BY CLIVE BRUNSKILL

Game, Set, Championship

Pete Sampras, 1997 (above)

PHOTOGRAPH BY CLIVE BRUNSKILL

(Opposite, clockwise from top left)

Virginia Wade, 1977; Billie Jean King, right, with Maria Bueno, 1968; Pete Sampras, 1997;
Ann Jones, 1969; Andre Agassi, 1992; Pat Cash, 1987; Jana Novotna, 1998;
Jimmy Connors, 1974; Evonne Goolagong, 1971; Stefan Edberg, 1988; Steffi Graf, 1988;
Boris Becker, 1989; Martina Navratilova, 1990; Bjorn Borg, 1976

PHOTOGRAPHS ALLSPORT, AND THE ALLSPORT HISTORICAL COLLECTION © HULTON GETTY

~ the winners ~

Visions of Wimbledon

The photographs in this book have been selected from the
extensive Wimbledon library of Allsport, the world's leading sports picture agency.
The photographs and their availability in all corners of the world
would not have been possible without the help of the following:
The Photographers, Picture Researchers, Darkroom Staff,
Picture Desk Operators, Accounts Staff, Clerical Staff
and everyone else in the Allsport offices at

ALLSPORT (UK) LTD
3 Greenlea Park
Prince George's Road
London SW19 2JD

Tel: (0208) 685 1010 • Fax: (0208) 648 5240
contact: Lee Martin   e-mail: lmartin@allsport.co.uk

ALLSPORT PHOTOGRAPHY USA INC
Allsport Building,
17383 Sunset Boulevard,
Pacific Palisades,
California 90272-4191

Tel: (310) 230 3400 • Fax: (310) 573 7600
contact: Greg Walker   e-mail: gwalker@allsport.com

ALLSPORT NEW YORK
8/3 Broadway, Suite 500,
New York, NY 10003

Tel: (212) 979 0903 Fax: (212) 979 0460
contact: Peter Orlowsky   e-mail: porlowsky@allsport.com

ALLSPORT AUSTRALIA
38 Atchison Street
St Leonards, NSW 2065, Australia

Tel: (612) 9460 7700 • Fax: (612) 9460 7711
contact: Dave Maher   e-mail: davem@allsport.com

ALLSPORT MELBOURNE
Ground Floor, 108 Ireland Street
West Melbourne, Victoria 3003, Australia

Tel: (613) 9329 2344 • Fax: (613) 9329 0405
contact: Tony Feder   e-mail: feder@allsport.com

AGENCE VANDYSTADT/ALLSPORT FRANCE
115 Rue De Vaugirard
75015 Paris, France

Tel: (01) 56 585757 Fax: (01) 56 585758
contact: Alain Danino   e-mail agence.vandystadt@wanadoo.fr

ALLSPORT WEBSITE
http://www.allsport.com

ANDRE
DEUTSCH